The Purpose Behind My Pain Wouldn't Let Me Quit

Book Journal

BY MARTHA SHERILL

All rights reserved. No Part of this publication may be reproduced, stored in retrieval system, or transmitted in any form or by any means, electronic, mechanical, photocopying recording or otherwise, without the prior written permission of the author.

Unless otherwise noted, all scriptures quotations are from the HOLY BIBLE, ESV® NIV®, KJV VERSION ® unless otherwise noted

Copyright © 2021 Martha Sherill

Publisher Creamed Colored Publications

ISBN 978-0-9863178-7-3

Table of Contents

Dedication Page 4

Acknowledgements 5

Lack of Education, Does Not Stop A Determined Mind 7

The Becoming of Martha "Tha" Boss 12

Just Do It 16

Faking It Till You Make It 19

Pain Before Purpose 23

Looking For Love 26

Self Love Birthed Out of Pain 32

Don't Judge Me 34

Understanding the Assignment 37

Loss Can Cause Despair 44

Dedication Page

I would like to dedicate this book to my children and grandchildren. Through the good and bad times, you have been with me every step of the way. You all have been like pillars, helping to hold me up. In my darkest moments you gave me hope and inspiration to fight for my life and to never give up. I love you and thank you!

In Loving Memory Of
My Mother Mary
My Grandson Antonio
My Best Friend Chico

Although you all are not with me physically, you will always live in my heart and mind. I know that you all will be so proud of my accomplishments, keep watching over me.

Acknowledgements

My heartfelt love and gratitude to my children, family, my two besties, my friends, my Apostle, my mentors, my team, and my book coach, that has poured into me over the years. So many times, I wanted to give up, so many nights and days I've cried to God to send me genuine people in my life to help me and he did. When I didn't know the how, the what, or when to make certain moves, I needed to bring my vision into full manifestation, God used each of you to play key roles to helping me stay the course. I want to thank you all for your words of wisdom, prayers, and support.

Failure will never overtake me if my determination to succeed is strong enough.

Og Mandino

Lack of Education, Does Not Stop A Determined Mind

Life can be challenging and hard, but with the help of God and a well made-up mind can take you a long way. The Bible declares for if any man lack wisdom ask of God.

Many nights and days I had to cry and rely on people to help me until I learned how to rely on God and allow him to direct my way. I did not know exactly what the plan was for my life, but I knew I wanted more. In seeking God for help and direction of the unknown and my most difficult times, I knew if I endured through the process God had something greater awaiting me.

Pain, test, trials, and hardship is difficult to deal with, and it hurts so much. But if you lean and depend on God's unchanging hand and grace everything will run its course and all things shall work together for your good. 1Peter 5:10 will be made manifest...the glory that is to be reveal will not compare to the gory of all you had to go through. It was all necessary and apart of the process for me to breath and began to live life.

Just because you dropped out of high school is not what determines if you failed, the only one who can determine that you failed or what you will become is "you". I went through many years of my life a shame of the fact that I was a high school dropout. The person that others saw in me was totally different from the person I saw myself. The problem was I saw myself as a person that couldn't be in intellectual settings and speak or be as successful as those, I looked at to be successful. For me, I was just a single mom, with six children doing the best I could. my mindset was fragile, and my self-esteem was on life support. But I didn't die in the process, I continued to thrive and find myself a lifeline that enabled me to maintain a pulse. I say this because I made so many mistakes which led into many painful experiences, that held me mentally captive. Many days I wanted to give up, but my biggest why was not to see my kids go without and to see me give up. The purpose behind the pain, wouldn't let me quit. You will see me say this often as you read through the chapters. This is what you need to know what is your biggest why and the purpose behind you accomplishing your goals. My kids played a great role in keeping me with hope. Without a high School education, I was able to get a full-time job with the Miami Dade County School Board and I have worked there for over a decade in the Transportation Department.

My passion to be successful gave life to my purpose despite my pain, I refused to let it stop or block me from fulfilling my desire to live the best life that God has for me. I continue seeking God for direction and help.

Matthew 6:33 states, Seek ye first the Kingdom of God and all his righteousness and he shall give you the desire of your heart.

With that scripture being my guide, I kept searching the word of God and acknowledged Him in all I did. As I began to get closer to God, His presence became more real and with his leading, lead me to the right people and resources that I needed so that I may began to believe in myself and pick up the pieces that was missing so that I can see clear the blueprint God has for my life.

The fear of the unknown, for a lack of better words, lack of knowledge and most times was so powerful that I couldn't let my pain stop me from moving forward and living the life I longed for, so I kept searching for the answer. The first thing I needed to do was find a way to believe in myself again. Let's tackle vital components of your inner struggle: Is there negative self-talk, fear of trying new things, overeating, time-wasting, social media over-indulgence in your home, or close relationships?

When your back is against the wall and seems that all odds are against you, fear sets in. Then is when you must make up in your mind to face your fears or continue being defeated. I had to remind myself that God did not give me the spirit of fear, so I faced my fears, so that I could conquer anything that stood in my way. It was not an easy task because the more I moved passed one obstacle, other challenges came. However, the more I faced them, I began to conquer anxiety and lessen the stress that use to come along with the obstacles. I had a problem over thinking because of being afraid of losing, failure and disappointments. I would see my peers and others succeeding yet, I was so afraid because I didn't speak as they did, didn't feel I knew enough and I would contribute just enough to get me close to where I wanted to be, then hide by sitting on my hands, my voice, my full potential, and gift due fear of the lack of knowledge. My insecurities kept me stuck at a certain place. As a result of my fear, I went through a lot of wrong turns, ups and downs trying to obtain my goals. Many times came that I wanted to give up and quit, but I knew my purpose was far bigger than me. I knew that my Why was bigger than my fears, and that all things would soon work out for my good if I didn't quit. Through my coaching and mentoring session help me to realize that for me to be successful as I desired that I had to begin to understand my purpose. I had to learn to endure hardness as good soldier so that I can be able to stand up in the midst of adversity. With that being said, with God help gave me a voice for others, showing them how God did it for me and that he can also do it for them.

Despite what it looks like or what others may be saying, or may try to do to discourage you, if you will stay focus, you will be okay. Staying focused, sometimes was my hardest task. You have to learn how to block all manner of distractions in order to stay on course with your vision. I had to learn people are cruel and going to be negative at times. So, with that, I learned people places and things beyond my control I will not continue to allow it to dictate the course of my life.

I learned to function in faking it all while failing miserably. It was times in my life that I was so into my outer appearance and what I thought being successful looked like, all at the same time losing sight and created more losses then wins, more obstacles than success for myself.

When you allow people places or things to resonate within your mindset it does nothing more than cause distractions, pain, and delayed progress.

Learn to invest in yourself, make a conscious decision to change your mindset and make a lifestyle change. What I am suggesting is that you add daily to your life to increase the chances of your success. I invested in myself, sought help, and obtain a coach and mentors that held me accountable.

Seek help, this will be a great start to helping you jump start your path to success. This investment helped me grow and gain confidence. I am fulfilling my dream building my business and my team. It took me first investing in myself so that I could be educated, empowered, and strengthened in order for me to start walking in my purpose. I Didn't think I could accomplish what I saw so many others had accomplished. I was so fearful and afraid thinking I would fail. Because of the limiting beliefs and lack of confidence, I was accepting failure. I figured because I dropped out of school, because many failed attempts at trying to do things to better myself didn't work, I began to allow doubt to set in.

Because of that, many years I counted myself out by having the wrong mindset. I thank God for sending the right people in my life at the right time to help build and encourage me and held me accountable. I prayed and asked God for courage and to help me and he did just that. It took me some time to get my loco motor time to speed up but, with the help of others keeping me accountable and praying to God for strength, such a calm came over me and my level of self-confidence increased and my passion to thrive was greater than I had ever seen. I began to become bold and take charge over my fears of what I did not know and went full throttle with what I knew and my strengths outweighed my weaknesses.

"Stay true to your brand and true to your voice and audiences will respond to that authenticity with enthusiasm and passion."

Kevin Spacey

The Becoming of Martha "Tha" Boss

I had to identify with my gift and talent, and with the help of my coaches and mentors, the gift was being stirred up on the inside. I had to realize that if I wanted to be as successful as I said, I had to Boss up, know my worth, know who I was and where I was trying to go, was critical steps that I needed to take in order to level up.

When I began to be true to myself, not afraid of what I lack, and confident in what I did know, I can honestly say by faith and the help of God lights began to come on in dark places, doors began to open that was once closed. All I could say is nobody but God.

Listen when I tell you when the purpose behind your pain is greater than you, it will not allow you to quit. I stop doubting my ability and start relying on God capabilities. Just because we don't see the full blueprint is not enough to stop or give up. Our faith in God, and trust in his guidance will lead us to a successful end. Your passion will push you to keep going, regardless of obstacles that comes, you still push because deep down inside you know in your heart you deserve more.

I stopped living through someone else dream, I had to break the cycle of fear and start to pursue my own. The more I began to believe in myself and study the course I was on is when I was able to focus on my strength and not allow my weakness to kill the hidden treasures inside of me.

Let me tell you I worked many long hours as a school bus driver and I was grateful to God for my job and made a descent income and was comfortable, but I knew I wanted greater and better for myself and family. The desire and dream were so much bigger than me, but I remembered attending a seminar and the person say "if your dream doesn't scare you, it's not big enough" I was like what? It did not register right away what that meant. I will say if there is one thing, I took away from that seminar was that statement. I began to meditate and think about it, because if it's one thing that I know, is that what God had begun to do in my life was bigger than me and scary. So, I guess I had a dream and making it my reality was a work in progress that was being navigated by God. I asked for it and remember the last chapter I mention Matthew 6:33 Seek ye first the kingdom of God and all things shall be added. My vision became aligned with God and his purpose for my life and then my life began to flourish.

I knew God was with me and I had a vision to help others and build a team that we can all win together. I knew I needed help. I prayed and God answered. I saw the vision I just needed clarity on how it was supposed to come full circle. Becoming Martha "tha" boss wasn't an easy task for me. God had been showing me signs and sending people to confirm his word to me, I still did not readily accept that God was speaking to me.

I felt that I didn't have the knowledge it took to be successful and build my business let alone to write my first book. It took years before I yield and say God, I will follow you as you lead the way. My saying yes to God, brought such a calm over me as I began to boldly speak to myself affirmations to conquer silence the voice of negative thoughts and any assignment of distractions. When you make up your mind to focus on your vision instead of others, you will lose friends, family and colleagues once they realize they can no longer use you, dictate to you or make you feel like you need them. One thing about God, he will never leave you, and will send new people to help you build solid in your business. I took some time for me to grasp all of what was happening within my circle, I had to realize my vision did not have to be align with what other people envisioned for me. I was stuck in mediocre and settled with where I was. However, when I made a conscious decision to step out on faith with a full-time job also building and owning my own business, I heard God say I will be the head and not the tail, the lender and not the borrower. I began to think different and speak different and could literally see myself walking into my wealthy place mentally, physically, and financially. In order for that to happen I had begun to understand my assignment. I had to be truthful to myself and face the facts that I had to take some major steps towards my goal and towards building a strong team. When opportunity came, I embraced it, and worked my butt off because I was finally in a place I had been waiting for a long time. I had to understand knowing my goal and what areas I needed help and stay focused.

What I will say here is I thank God and I thank God for all my support systems. It was all necessary for building my business and in the discovery of becoming Martha "Tha" Boss. Many nights I cried out praying to God send me genuine people and leaders to help cultivate my life and when He did, He showed out. I had to stop allowing negative people to speak negativity in my spirit and seek God to send people that could not only speak into my spirit positive reinforcement but that could pour into me that I may accomplish my dreams and making a reality.

If you feel like there's something out there that you're supposed to be doing, if you have a passion for it, then stop wishing and just do it.

Wanda Sykes

Just Do It

Don't procrastinate about fulfilling your dream. We are given just one opportunity at life, so whatever your desire is in life, it is solely and entirely up to you to make it happen. Your next level to advance is going to be critical. You will have to understand who you really are, being honest and true to yourself, and not allowing your emotions to get in your way. Now is your opportune time to get started working on your dreams. I know how it feels not knowing the full step to take to venture out but have faith and trust in God that he has equipped you with the necessary resources and tools to be successful.

When you don't know what your next step will be, seek help. Never allow what you don't know be the reason you don't pursue your goal. One day I came home from the office, and I did not understand what was to happen next with my business, I was so desperate for change, all I could do is fall down on my knees and cry out to God I need help. I knew it was so much more I needed.

I had a burning desire to make a difference, in building up other young ladies that have a dream, but their vision had been obscured by broken promises, broken relationships, gave up on themselves. I wanted to be the one to encourage them to just do it. If Nike can inspire the world with that concept, I believed that I could inspire my readers and the young ladies that has come into my life.

As I began to help these women, the word of God was released to me that by me helping those that was apart of my team, by creating a platform for them to build, that I was setting the blaze to create millionaires. I accepted this word. This word encouraged me to push harder, not only am I generating wealth for myself and family but now I am helping others generate generational wealth as well. My faith kept on leaping, each accomplishment achieved, I was on to the next. I would affirm myself and speak to myself you can do this Martha, you were born for this, just do it.

Looking back or giving up at this point in my life was far from my mind. It just didn't make much sense, looking at what God has allowed me to accomplish, I knew in order for me to remain successful quitting was not the way.

Dare to be successful, put in the work, be passionate about it and once you do the strength you need will snatch you from your comfort zone. Your hunger has to roar louder than your fear. It will be a challenge but follow your dreams, command yourself to act on it by faith, so you can make your dream become your now.

In the meantime, the clock is ticking, don't waste any time thinking about what's impossible, think about how you can make your dream possible.

The key is you must make up your mind that you won't allow the negativity, past mistakes, and pain stop you. In fact, all of those should be motivating factors that causes you to want to go hard, sometimes our best efforts and success will come from our deepest times of tribulation and adversities. If you want success as bad as you want to breathe, remember no one can make this happen for you like you. If it is fear that's standing in your way, then be encouraged.....defeat your F-E-A-R and just do it ! I learned that fear is only the False-Evidence-of things-Appearing-Real.

"So as a man think in his heart, so is he."
Proverbs 23:7

Continue to think that you can and so shall it be. You must remember it is not about what others feels, think or say, it is what you think and believe about yourself.

"Don't let peer pressure and expectations drive you to live above your means."

Dave Ramsey

Faking It Till You Make It

Never judge a book by its cover as the old saying goes. Many like to look at a person and assume that because they see that person dress good, looking good, driving a nice car, and living nice that life is like a bowl full of cherries. Let me help some of you out, it's the saying fake it until you make it, that'll have you exhausted and frustrated. I have always been conscious about keeping myself up, making sure my hygiene and appearance was good. Looking the part but money did not match my appetite. I had a good job, and I started my own business, making extra income, but my priorities were not in order as they should've been, therefore my finances weren't enough for my tastebuds, my appetite was greater than my budget. I went from faking it till I make it, to prioritizing, budgeting, and balancing both which enabled me to live the life I desire and deserved.

I was living from paycheck to paycheck, robbing Peter to pay Paul. I became a regular customer at all the local pawn shops pawning my jewelry, I was the queen of pay day advances trying to keep up with my habit of having luxurious things that I really could not afford while entertaining others. I bought myself lavish gifts instead of paying my bills on time or before the due date, Instead I would pay the bare minimum or pay nothing at all and ask for an extension

I know I am not the only one that has crossed this bridge. If you have been faking it until you make it, it's time to do some rearranging to prioritizing your lifestyle. It's okay to look the part but look it responsibly. Most of what I was dealing with was a direct reflection of my poor choices, Poor money management. If this sounds familiar to you and you are still faking it then allow this to encourage you, being you, shouldn't almost cost you, yourself. Don't' misunderstand me, you deserve to enjoy your life.

But if you are struggling and failing, often it's because you have chosen to live above what your bank account says. If this sounds like your story and situation, then this message is for you.

Despite your comfort zone, that you may be in right now, it is my prayer that my testimony will provoke you to get pass your obstacles, limiting beliefs and run with your vision. Don't allow the pain of your past, lack or fear cause you to forfeit your purpose. Your purpose has a mission, and you are responsible for making it happen for you. My journey is just begun, yet through the help of my team, mentors, my pastor, my kids, my visions, and dreams are now my reality.

I was dealing with so much, dealing with life's issues caused me to mask my truth, while trying to fill a void and feed my pain with substance that had temporary relief. which led me to me to failure, rejections, frustrations and repeating the same cycles repeatedly. It took me realizing that success is not about how successful you look, or how popular you may seem, but the peace in knowing that my purpose was being fulfilled solely in helping others, helped me realized it was more to investing and sustaining wealth and more so what success looked like for me. I had to learn what it takes to be as successful as others that I followed, that's successful in doing what I desire.

It took some years of being discipline, humiliated, highs, lows before discovering the diamond in the ruff. The faceoff is, you will be challenged on the journey to success, but I want to encourage you to keep pushing past those obstacles of fear that surely will come, in the form of doubt, negative people, self-sabotage (I can't, lack of self-confidence, low self-esteem) You have to silence the voice of negativity and know that the purpose behind the pain is far greater than your obstacles. Get up dust yourself off and speak positive affirmations over your life and ask God to lead you to divine connections via mentors or networks that will educate you and push you to your next level.

Believe and be encouraged and know that you can and will achieve anything if you really want it and put your mind to it, you shall accomplish your goals and dreams. One of the hardest parts of this journey can be to own up to your mistakes and take responsibility for why you are where you are right now. Time to stop making excuses and we must take responsibility for what we allow to happen and unapologetically take your life back and boldly go after your dreams.

The experience is costly, but if you get the lesson the benefit of passing the test is so much more rewarding mentally, physically, and financially. As you utilize this journal, I pray you write your vision, dream and desires to help bring clarity in your life.

"You may have had unfair things happen to you, but the depth of your pain is an indication of the height of your future."

Joel Osteen

Pain Before Purpose

When your back is against the wall, and it seems that all odds are against you, fear will set in. In this instance, you must make up your mind to face what you fear or continue being defeated.

I had to remind myself that God did not give me the spirit of fear, so I faced my fears, so that I could conquer anything that stood in my way. It was not an easy task because the more I moved past one obstacle more challenges seem to come. However, as I faced them, I began to conquer the anxiety, and lessen the stress that was always there along with the obstacles.

The journey was not easy and to this day I am still experiencing the challenges, that may come in the form of some type of pain, or it may be associated with disappointment. Let me share something with that you should always remember. "Depending on others and negativity is the blueprint for disappointment."

When those trigger Points come and have me thinking negative thoughts, for instance things like you're not going to make it, this is not your calling, it's not your time, or its too difficult and too hard for you to conquer, you'll never make it. I had to overcome that negativity by feeding it with positive affirmations and with the word of God. For example, one of my favorite verses that I would rely on was "I can do all things through Christ who strengthens me, and in him will I trust to lead and guide me when all else seems to fail."

As painful as things were, I learned over time how to stay focused, and I realized that my thoughts can and will ultimately be the determining factor of how my life would turn out, be it good or bad. Journaling became therapy for me. Unable to confide in others, about my sincerest and deepest thoughts, and my pain. I would find myself talking to God as I mentioned before. In this I found it to be liberating to write about what I was experiencing. No matter what your pain is, I hope that I can encourage other women who are faced with the same or similar circumstances and challenges. I'll leave you with this; that no matter the challenge, NEVER GIVE UP!

"People make the mistake of entering into a relationship and thinking that the other person will fill the void that they are missing, that they will bring them the happiness and joy they are looking for."

Hagir Elsheikh

Looking For Love

As I grew up, I saw love within my family. I thought I knew love in relationships I embraced only to realize as I became an adult it was not the love I knew of growing. As I grew up, I began dating and establishing friendships that to me was ideal and quite fun but came with a lot of pain and emotions. I endured a roller coaster ride of relationships over the course of my life, and with some the pain continued through the mistreatments, betrayals, and deception. It took some time to realize that what I had accepted as Love was not love. Especially when I had been taught that love is supposed to be kind, gentle, and protecting.

Although my mother had always instilled in me good morals, principles and good conduct. As I grew older and began to attract boys. the attention I received felt flattering. I started growing fond of the attention and didn't heed the warnings of my momma like many of us do and before I knew it I was seeking that affection in a relationship with a guy from around the neighborhood. I began to accept his concept of what love was, I was young and gullible and wanted to belong. I wanted to be apart of the trend. Unaware and without experience, I had no idea of what was ahead for me.

In time I was exposed to the good, the bad and most of all, the ugly. Let's just say. This was one of those rides I hopped on that I now wished I would have listened to momma and not have taken a seat on the roller coaster of love. But as the saying goes, it's too late. It wasn't until many years later that I realized that this was not love, it was only an illusion. It turned out to be more of a nightmare than a dream, or the fairytale that I'd been hoping for.

Over the years I searched for love only to continue to experience one disappointment after the next. Blind love is the recipe for heartbreak.

Sadly, I stayed in the few relationships I had longer than I should have. I was looking for love in not just the wrong places but in the wrong people from a mate, friends, and some business relations. As it relates to dating, seemingly instead of a match made in heaven, it felt more like a match sent from hell. It went from a great start to abuse verbally, then physically and to stripping me mentally.

My emotions were all over the place. I hadn't realized all the pain that was attached to this fantasy, or what I thought was love.

One of my biggest problems I dealt with is I did not know how to let go and out of fear accepted a replica of love. I was scared, I was a young a single mother raising my kids, with some help from their father. I Thank God for my mother playing intricate role in helping me in every step of the way

Fast forward, I survived passed a lot of the hurt and pain of my past, but never gave up on love, still was willing to give it a try. I spent years dating someone, who was introduced to me by mutual associates. From the introductions, resulted in a relationship that turned out to be not what God had for me, even though I stayed in the relationship longer than I should have. He turned out to be an excellent liar, and a constant cheater and on top of that he was dating someone else during which time we dated and to then turn around and without my knowledge goes and secretly get married, all while we were still dating. Sadly, it did not bother him being a narcissistic through the whole ordeal. Me thinking God not another blow.

Although the pain was deep, I couldn't do anything but cry, turn to God, repent and thank him for embracing me. God was trying to get my attention long time ago and I ignored the signs. I needed to know love and when I began to build my relationship with God, He began to reveal His love to me and what love is. As I begin to grow in God's word the closer my relationship became with Him and the more, He showed His love to me through many different channels of love. God sent help through his faithful servants that had been through similar problems, that shared their life experiences to help get me through my situation.

Being a single mom, I often wondered how I would make it. I went through many nights feeling broken and rejected. I cried many days and nights. growing up with lack of confidence and broken, that same broken young lady became a broken woman still lacking the attention and love she longed to have. still lacking the attention and love she longed to have. It came to my attention, that I was always giving and always investing more in others and thinking about how others felt about me rather than how I should've been feeling and thinking of myself.

I was Giving of myself, my heart and love, because by nature I am a giver and I thought that if I did that, it would make my relationships better and that they will love me, because of my expression of love towards them. Boy was I wrong.

As I write this it seems quite strange but in remembrance of my past it seems I was always eager and always willing to give and wanted nothing more than to be loved back in relationships. I had to learn that people you love may not love you back the way you love them. I am sure I don't have to tell you, but the pain of an abusive and failed relationship will cause one to be leery and afraid to meet new people and engage in a new relationship.

Many gave me their input and their advice, Martha you deserve better, you don't have to take the mental abuse. It just seemed easier said than done. Having to muscle up the courage to step out of a relationship you thought was solid. I knew it was a decision that I had to make, just seemed a bit harder to leave.

So many young women, that I have spoken with have been in the same situation that I was in and at some point, based their self-worth and value on the measurement of what other expected from them and of them.

That saying holds true, it is always someone that may be experiencing the same thing or maybe worse than you. I was an empty soul longing for something real, something to fill the void. I had to stop for a moment and stop looking for people's validation and start seeking God for direction and fulfilling the void and not from others. You either going to seek God after hitting rock bottom with your search and acknowledge him that he may give you the desires of your heart. God can connect you with the right people, resources, and place you in the right relationships if you would allow him to lead you.

Listen many times after saying I was done with a relationship, I found myself letting my guards down and going back to what I knew was not good for me hoping to God that individual or person had change. Because they would call, pleading and saying they were sorry, I would walk back into the trap, thinking this time it would be different. I had to become numb and sick of accepting less than what I deserved. When I became truly broken and cried out to God, He heard my cry.

The brokenness of love and trust did not only stem from a dating relationship but also from some family relationships, business relationships, and some personal relationships. I had to ask God to help me to accept the facts of how people feel or are that I move on and not gracefully and love from a distance if that is best. In time past I would answer the calls listen to the lies and the false apologies and allow people back in my life, but when I found myself loosing me again, I had to start ignoring calls, asking myself why, would I want people like that back, all the pain and hurt outweighed the good. I can remember in time past I was so broken as a woman, that I thought pain was a part of love.

I had to understand self-love and self-gratitude. God had to teach me how to love myself before He bring someone else in my life. This time I have a better understanding of what love looks like and feel like because God has allowed me to experience his love and self-love. When I began to seek a stronger and closer relationship with God, He began to show me his unconditional love. I began to see my true worth through Christ and realized the greatest love of all is His love for mankind and not predicated on the love from any one person or in any unhealthy relationships rather it's business or personally.

The lack of value on myself was diluted and masked by dressing up and adorning my outside appearance. Don't make the mistakes I made being broken and looking for love in all the wrong people, things, as I was blinded by a replica of love.

"Love yourself so much that when others come around you, they either step up or step aside."

Marion Bekoe

Self Love Birthed Out of Pain

The beauty within, is to be discovered and I had to discover something that I have looked for in others practically all my life. I looked for love in all the wrong people, only to realize it had to start within me first. I allowed people feelings to override my true feeling and suffered emotionally, trying to not to see others hurt. This is the worst ever, you are slowing suffocating and dying and allowing others to live and thrive at the expense of sacrificing yourself. You talk about miserable, but in the midst of it all I kept right on smiling, laughing and inwardly hurting.

Toxic Relationships cost so much in the long run. You have to muscle up strength and use it to transform your life. I know I can say it now but a few years back I could not muscle up enough strength to say it nor see that certain relationships just weren't good for me. I do believe you too when to that place in your life that you are tired, then is when you will begin to declare enough is enough mindset and the tenacity to walk away from toxic relationships. I have experienced many years of abuse mentally, physically, and verbally from others I gave permission. Yes, I gave permission. I did nothing about it, said nothing about it. Kept it a secret, because I did not know what love was and too afraid to be alone. It becomes worse not better, I did not know my self-worth, and did not have self-confidence to get out. Unfortunately, most of us that is in relationships like this have an obscure view of what love is.

"Don't concern yourself with the opinions of those who judge you. That is placing on them an importance they do not have."

Donna Lynn Hope

Don't Judge Me

People will judge you based on how you grew up, what you wear, how you look, how much money you have, or your background. Years I went through life feeling purposeless not knowing who I really was, having self-doubts, jumping on band wagon after band wagon only to discover that was not a part of the plan of God for me. Take all paths as lessons, learn from them, use what you need and leave the rest behind on a what not to do list. Don't allow it to deter you from growing and moving forward. I have always desired of making a difference in my life and my family. Despite all the good I had done or do some people will still bring up my past arrest, fights, wrong decisions and misunderstandings with people that I had experienced in my life. In spite of those that judged me, I had to learn how to not let it affect my growth and move forward. I desired to be the forerunner and make a difference in my home, business and to strive after greater things then what I had. The one thing that stopped me was the fear of people and what they would think if I failed or did something wrong. Before I would try or even think that I could, I had already disqualified myself based on my fear of being judged. The craziest thought for me is I could see the success for others, but I couldn't see me achieving that level of success. I would push and help others with funding and fulfilling their dreams all while sabotaging mines. I wanted more for others then I wanted for myself. Although I was hurting in secret, I did not want others to know so I found a hidden place in showing up for others, blended looking as if in the presence of the celebration I was being looked upon as one of the successful ones.

I had to release fear because holding on to it became like kryptonite was to superman. It was not till I began to have confidence that I began to experience freedom I needed to reach my goals and live my dreams. I had to learn to change my mindset or remain in captive inside the prison walls of my mind. Stop allowing people to imprisoned you by fear of what they may think or say about your dream.

Stop focusing in on what happens if I fail? What about focusing on What if I am successful? I had to realize if I never try to do, what I desire to do, I will never know if I could do it and if I fail, I did two things I tried, and I gain experience. With those two things I gain enough to not give up but to try again now with a little more confidence and experience on what not to do that I did the first time. It may cost you, but remember whatever the cost, in the end you will be able to look back and see it was well worth the effort then simply giving up. Life is meant to be lived purposely and will at times cause us to stretch and push beyond what we believe we could possibly handle.

I change the way in which I looked at things and it change my life.

In order to grow, sometimes you will be faced with adversities, but I knew that I had to continue to push beyond the breaking point of giving up and being judge by people.

"Understanding is deeper than knowledge, there are many people who may know you but there are very few who understand you"

Unknown

Understanding the Assignment

I was a teen mom struggling and at the time I did not have the maternal skills to balance raising children and balancing my life.

In addition to that, there was always a need for constant support and internal growth. And because of my short comings, I encountered so many situations and challenges as my life seem to collide head-on with so many major changes. Thanking God, with help, that over the years, I learned and overcame the challenges.

Fast forward, when I began to seek God about starting my own business...once again my training days started all over again.

For me to give birth to starting a new business I had to be willing to endure the birthing pains that comes with the assignment. I equally believed for me to make my dream a reality it was going to take my total concentration and focus. I had to keep my dream at the forefront of my desire. I could not afford to lose, it was either I win or fail and because my decision did not just include me, but my children as well. I had to win. This gamble taught me about the "power" in a decision.

As I continued to communicate with my Mentor, she would always stress this particular point; "Your attitude determines your altitude." I didn't realize at first what that meant, honestly, I just agreed by saying okay, I get it. You must change your attitude and take control of your emotions and focus on what does your vision regarding how you see yourself on the next level looked. She would say you can't see the positivity or the height of your success with the wrong mindset. She would assign me what seem like tons of homework, that required that I also do research, and some inner searching.

Truthfully, I was focused on what I believed to be success in the lives of other people rather than figuring out my own path for what success would be for me.

Once I understood my assignment and became focused on what keeping the grass green on my side of things meant, I began to see the results that I desired in my business. And in doing this, I also experience growth. This is what I learned; "Sometimes in life you have to take a step back for a major comeback, and every now and then, you have to experience the ultimate breakdown to experience the "Ultimate Breakthrough."

Don't be afraid of what you don't know or don't have. Just as I shared It was a lot, I did not know about being a teenage mom and giving birth to six healthy kids at an early age, I had to seek help, same with my business. I knew how to hustle and had to realize it was more to running a successful business.

The key here is that I was willing to be a student and learn the things that I lacked; Whether it was knowledge that I did not have, or the skill set that I needed for me to be successful.

I received help from several business coaches and mentors in the areas that I needed. The trainings and teachings help me stay accountable and to set obtainable goals for myself and my business. Having the proper structure, I am able to multitask and find balance within my businesses, making several streams of income.

Investing in business coaching, I was able to stay on course prioritizing goals in a timely manner instead of trying to accomplish several things at one time, which end up most of my task being incomplete or lacking.

I want to share with you three additional components that I acquired along the way.

1. Make sure you set your goals.

2. Create an Action Plan

3. Set a Timeline

Once I understood the assignment, I began to focus more on what I wanted and how I planned to get there. I learned how to create a road map to reach my goal.

As a professional bus driver, if there is one thing that I knew from experience was knowing how to create a step-by-step set of directions of how I would arrive at each stop on my bus route.

As my coach would often say what you want, desire or dreaming for, does not have any planned actions in place then it is not a goal.

Instead of focusing on what I did not know, or have I begun to focus on what I had and what I did know and daily add to my action plan by doing research on the goal at hand. It seems that what I had was desires but not realistically a goal. When I understood the assignment of having goals it increased the chances of me having what I dreamed, wanted or desire was now clearer and more obtainable.

This helped me to gain momentum when my goals begin to align with my vision. I believe that, basically you can't achieve your goal if you don't know how you will arrive at achieving it.

I wasted many years of my life missing out on many opportunities because of the fear of not feeling ready or that I was not good enough. I continued to self-doubt myself and it placed me in a self-imposed prison. It took me awhile to see that others who are successful were no different than me. I began to realize the difference was I accepted the self-sabotaging tactics. I just didn't think that I had what it takes it seemed like all the odds was against me. thinking so negatively kept me stuck in a place just enough to get by. So, I had to give myself a reality check. My mind-set had to change, how I responded to opposition had to change, but most of all how I reacted to adversity had to change absolutely. My emotions were all over the place.

A fair warning after you set goals, you're going to encounter some hiccups with your vision, trust me before I understood my assignment, I was no stranger to failures from failed relationships from failed friendships from failed businesses because I doubted myself and allowed fear to get the best of me. I hope that I encourage you not to give up because there's purpose behind your pain. Get up and start that business and start over if you must. One thing, I will share I don't regret any of my experiences. I'll have you to know, not one grain of your past experiences is ever wasted. Experience is sometimes your best teacher.

When I understood my assignment fear no longer gripped me, it created a craving within me and a hunger to reach my goal, and at the same time it created in me a desire to see my dreams to be successful come true.

Afraid of failure is one of the most common fears we can have; for example, I would say to myself, "I'll look crazy, or what will others think about me or what will they say?"

You start questioning yourself, talk back to your fears and start speaking about what you have accomplished and apply the same energy and actions towards each goal you set.

I endured pains, and delays. There were days that I wanted to give up, but with God's help and in addition to me staying focused, I acquired enough knowledge and strength to endure and overcome every obstacle to get where I am today. I can't explain exactly why life happened the way that it did, but I do know if I would've given up long time ago, I will never be able to share my story with you and share with you that you can make it just like I did.

I was willing to try daily and add to what I was lacking. When you get a sincere desire to make improvements in your life, your vision becomes priority. I can remember wanting to start a business and be good at it, but I really did not know how and had no real long-term goal, only from a hustling mentality without any real structure. I thought I was the big stuff. I would pay my way, get others to help me, pay for courses but was becoming overloading with everyone else's success track record, and not my own. I had to stop going and eating from every table and start preparing my own. I found it challenging for me to apply any knowledge I was getting because I never took time to lay my blueprint and use what I was learning for my business.

Self-doubt is your worst enemy it will have you second guessing yourself. Your will to succeed has to be greater than your fears. I had to literally get out of my own way. I had to finally realize that I was my biggest hinderance and I could no longer make excuses. I believe that a lot of what prolonged my being successful is my lack of knowledge and anxiety.

So much can come into play when pursuing your dreams. In operating in faith, you must trust God beyond what you see or feel in the natural. I encourage you to step out on faith and when you do you must trust God through the process despite of any circumstances and fears. Faith is the substance of things hoped for and the evidence of things not seen. Please know your faith will be tested that's why it's important to be patient and to work towards your goal knowing that faith without work or efforts is dead. Being a person of faith, I begin to Look back over my life and personal experiences of how I had to activate my faith by learning how to decree and declare God's word over my life.

I began to speak God word and declarations. I will stand on the promises of God and not on my own thoughts. I will keep my eyes focused on my goals and not lose hope. I will continue to trust, in God and not become distracted. I shall remain focused and know that God is the Author and the finisher of my faith. This was my attitude in affirming myself to make it all the way through my assignments.

My Mentor began to ask me certain questions about what I desired to do, and what skills I possessed. I began to share with her, and she said to me, said to me, Martha, you have a many gifts and talents within you, it's time to use what you have before adding to it. It may take some time, disciplining, and sacrificing in order for you to discover the gems, but don't stop searching. Over time I allowed the troubles of life and its distractions to distort my view and delay my purpose. In search and in the discovery process I went through many delays and some moments of despair, yet I continued to push through all the noise, the disappointments, being talked about and the misunderstandings. I had to remember that in the midst of the pain I was enduring had purpose. All I can hear in my head my momma saying shorty (my nick name), you must stay focus on your goals baby, don't be so hard on yourself.

I could not stop if I wanted change for the better to happen in my life. I know I had to provide a way for myself and family. I had to stop sacrificing myself trying to please others. put my best foot forward and try and live up to my true potential and do what I love doing. As I was healing, I met so many people that were scared, hurting, broken, frustrated, and discontented to the point of wanting to give up. These were people that I would have never suspected of being afraid of pursuing their dreams, to start a business or to just simply take the first step toward their vision. All I could do is be reminded of the times when I was semi-paralyzed in my own fear just as they were, and so I began to encourage them as my Mentor had with me. She would quite often say, "Just do it" scared. You have a natural gift about you Martha". "You are the only reason that you are not successful." You must want to see your dream come true more than your fear wants you to fail.

The struggle you are in today is developing the strength you need for tomorrow."

Robert Tew

Loss Can Cause Despair

When you lose things in life, sometimes it is hard to bury the lost and move on. I don't want to come across as having a pity party, but I went through some dark times and moments of despair in my life. But God has always made a way of escape for me. Trust me, when the bibles say, that God will always leave a ram in the bush "believe it." I am living proof that He will. It's because of that kind of evidence in the previous chapter I shared how I have always gone to God asking him for help and to place the right people in my life that would help me and not judge me. Please understand that in life we are going to be faced with some good times and bad times, but God will be never mis-lead you, and nor will He ever forsake you. Trust me when I tell you that.

Charles Dickens wrote it best. "It was the best of times, it was the worst of times, it was the age of wisdom, it was the age of foolishness, it was the epoch of belief, it was the epoch of incredulity, it was the season of light, it was the season of darkness, it was the spring of hope, it was the winter of despair, we had everything before us, we had nothing before us, we were all going direct to heaven, we were all going direct the other way–in short, the period was so far like the present period, that some of its noisiest authorities insisted on its being received, for good or for evil, in the superlative degree of comparison only".

~ A Tale of Two Cities

In speaking with a close friend about what I was feeling after the loss of my mother, my grandson, and my best friend, not to mention many other personal things, my loss was more than I could bare that left me in a state of despair.

She expressed to me how she had dealt with similar tragedies, and grief because of losing her mother and father weeks apart she was able to cope with her experiences and loses. Surprisingly, her testimony, tenacity and words of encouragement helped me get through some really tough times in my life, even suicidal.

Pain is one experience we all wished that we could live without. Pain comes in many forms and fashions, from tragedies, death, and circumstances that can push you beyond limits. So, I learned I could never underestimate a person's pain because I don't know their purpose. Everyone does not know how to help someone in pain nor realize that person's need for help is vital, unless of course it happens to them. Some feels as if I got over mines, they need to get over it already. The reality of that is every body process and deal with things differently.

As I have been encouraged, I hope you are being encouraged as you read my book. Although I was not alone, I felt abandon. There was a time when we were speaking that she quoted something to me that sounded like something I once read in the bible in the book of Ecclesiastes, chapter three. "There is a time and season for every purpose under the sun.

It was one thing I realized that these words were certainly a part of my reality and had given me hope to recognize that this was only for a season. I had to learn to see beyond my present state of mind and circumstances.

Even in the midst of depression, tears and heartache, I stayed praying and reading my bible more and trusting God with my process. I began focusing on the good in all the things that I had lost especially in comparison with God written word in Ecclesiastes, my faith began to be ignited and I regained sight of my purpose and my healing process begin. It was then I was able to start re-building.

Life is filled with ups and downs and with it comes lessons that we must learn. I had to understand this phase in my life that I had a choice to get up or stay in the dumps having a pity party.

So, I learned that I had to find the balance between what had been good times and the worst of times while keeping in mind the word of God. And in doing so, in my mind I could hear the words of my mom saying; "Shorty I told you, there were going to be days like this." I will be honest with you getting through those days, is like finding the needle in a haystack. Since I have deepened my relationship with

God, He has given me clarity and purpose behind my pain, that I may help others heal, using my experience as a living testimony. Although, it is no one size fit all, but the process will teach you how to stand strong even in the midst of adversity.

2022 calender

January
Su	Mo	Tu	We	Th	Fr	Sa
26	27	28	29	30	31	1
2	3	4	5	6	7	8
9	10	11	12	13	14	15
16	17	18	19	20	21	22
23	24	25	26	27	28	29
30	31	1	2	3	4	5

February
Su	Mo	Tu	We	Th	Fr	Sa
30	31	1	2	3	4	5
6	7	8	9	10	11	12
13	14	15	16	17	18	19
20	21	22	23	24	25	26
27	28	1	2	3	4	5

March
Su	Mo	Tu	We	Th	Fr	Sa
27	28	1	2	3	4	5
6	7	8	9	10	11	12
13	14	15	16	17	18	19
20	21	22	23	24	25	26
27	28	29	30	31	1	2

April
Su	Mo	Tu	We	Th	Fr	Sa
27	28	29	30	31	1	2
3	4	5	6	7	8	9
10	11	12	13	14	15	16
17	18	19	20	21	22	23
24	25	26	27	28	29	30

May
Su	Mo	Tu	We	Th	Fr	Sa
1	2	3	4	5	6	7
8	9	10	11	12	13	14
15	16	17	18	19	20	21
22	23	24	25	26	27	28
29	30	31	1	2	3	4

June
Su	Mo	Tu	We	Th	Fr	Sa
29	30	31	1	2	3	4
5	6	7	8	9	10	11
12	13	14	15	16	17	18
19	20	21	22	23	24	25
26	27	28	29	30	1	2

July
Su	Mo	Tu	We	Th	Fr	Sa
26	27	28	29	30	1	2
3	4	5	6	7	8	9
10	11	12	13	14	15	16
17	18	19	20	21	22	23
24	25	26	27	28	29	30
31	1	2	3	4	5	6

August
Su	Mo	Tu	We	Th	Fr	Sa
31	1	2	3	4	5	6
7	8	9	10	11	12	13
14	15	16	17	18	19	20
21	22	23	24	25	26	27
28	29	30	31	1	2	3

September
Su	Mo	Tu	We	Th	Fr	Sa
28	29	30	31	1	2	3
4	5	6	7	8	9	10
11	12	13	14	15	16	17
18	19	20	21	22	23	24
25	26	27	28	29	30	1

October
Su	Mo	Tu	We	Th	Fr	Sa
25	26	27	28	29	30	1
2	3	4	5	6	7	8
9	10	11	12	13	14	15
16	17	18	19	20	21	22
23	24	25	26	27	28	29
30	31	1	2	3	4	5

November
Su	Mo	Tu	We	Th	Fr	Sa
30	31	1	2	3	4	5
6	7	8	9	10	11	12
13	14	15	16	17	18	19
20	21	22	23	24	25	26
27	28	29	30	1	2	3

December
Su	Mo	Tu	We	Th	Fr	Sa
27	28	29	30	1	2	3
4	5	6	7	8	9	10
11	12	13	14	15	16	17
18	19	20	21	22	23	24
25	26	27	28	29	30	31

2023 calender

January
Su	Mo	Tu	We	Th	Fr	Sa
1	2	3	4	5	6	7
8	9	10	11	12	13	14
15	16	17	18	19	20	21
22	23	24	25	26	27	28
29	30	31	1	2	3	4

February
Su	Mo	Tu	We	Th	Fr	Sa
29	30	31	1	2	3	4
5	6	7	8	9	10	11
12	13	14	15	16	17	18
19	20	21	22	23	24	25
26	27	28	1	2	3	4

March
Su	Mo	Tu	We	Th	Fr	Sa
26	27	28	1	2	3	4
5	6	7	8	9	10	11
12	13	14	15	16	17	18
19	20	21	22	23	24	25
26	27	28	29	30	31	1

April
Su	Mo	Tu	We	Th	Fr	Sa
26	27	28	29	30	31	1
2	3	4	5	6	7	8
9	10	11	12	13	14	15
16	17	18	19	20	21	22
23	24	25	26	27	28	29
30	1	2	3	4	5	6

May
Su	Mo	Tu	We	Th	Fr	Sa
30	1	2	3	4	5	6
7	8	9	10	11	12	13
14	15	16	17	18	19	20
21	22	23	24	25	26	27
28	29	30	31	1	2	3

June
Su	Mo	Tu	We	Th	Fr	Sa
28	29	30	31	1	2	3
4	5	6	7	8	9	10
11	12	13	14	15	16	17
18	19	20	21	22	23	24
25	26	27	28	29	30	1

July
Su	Mo	Tu	We	Th	Fr	Sa
25	26	27	28	29	30	1
2	3	4	5	6	7	8
9	10	11	12	13	14	15
16	17	18	19	20	21	22
23	24	25	26	27	28	29
30	31	1	2	3	4	5

August
Su	Mo	Tu	We	Th	Fr	Sa
30	31	1	2	3	4	5
6	7	8	9	10	11	12
13	14	15	16	17	18	19
20	21	22	23	24	25	26
27	28	29	30	31	1	2

September
Su	Mo	Tu	We	Th	Fr	Sa
27	28	29	30	31	1	2
3	4	5	6	7	8	9
10	11	12	13	14	15	16
17	18	19	20	21	22	23
24	25	26	27	28	29	30

October
Su	Mo	Tu	We	Th	Fr	Sa
1	2	3	4	5	6	7
8	9	10	11	12	13	14
15	16	17	18	19	20	21
22	23	24	25	26	27	28
29	30	31	1	2	3	4

November
Su	Mo	Tu	We	Th	Fr	Sa
29	30	31	1	2	3	4
5	6	7	8	9	10	11
12	13	14	15	16	17	18
19	20	21	22	23	24	25
26	27	28	29	30	1	2

December
Su	Mo	Tu	We	Th	Fr	Sa
26	27	28	29	30	1	2
3	4	5	6	7	8	9
10	11	12	13	14	15	16
17	18	19	20	21	22	23
24	25	26	27	28	29	30
31	1	2	3	4	5	6

2024 calender

January
Su	Mo	Tu	We	Th	Fr	Sa
31	1	2	3	4	5	6
7	8	9	10	11	12	13
14	15	16	17	18	19	20
21	22	23	24	25	26	27
28	29	30	31	1	2	3

February
Su	Mo	Tu	We	Th	Fr	Sa
28	29	30	31	1	2	3
4	5	6	7	8	9	10
11	12	13	14	15	16	17
18	19	20	21	22	23	24
25	26	27	28	29	1	2

March
Su	Mo	Tu	We	Th	Fr	Sa
25	26	27	28	29	1	2
3	4	5	6	7	8	9
10	11	12	13	14	15	16
17	18	19	20	21	22	23
24	25	26	27	28	29	30
31	1	2	3	4	5	6

April
Su	Mo	Tu	We	Th	Fr	Sa
31	1	2	3	4	5	6
7	8	9	10	11	12	13
14	15	16	17	18	19	20
21	22	23	24	25	26	27
28	29	30	1	2	3	4

May
Su	Mo	Tu	We	Th	Fr	Sa
28	29	30	1	2	3	4
5	6	7	8	9	10	11
12	13	14	15	16	17	18
19	20	21	22	23	24	25
26	27	28	29	30	31	1

June
Su	Mo	Tu	We	Th	Fr	Sa
26	27	28	29	30	31	1
2	3	4	5	6	7	8
9	10	11	12	13	14	15
16	17	18	19	20	21	22
23	24	25	26	27	28	29
30	1	2	3	4	5	6

July
Su	Mo	Tu	We	Th	Fr	Sa
30	1	2	3	4	5	6
7	8	9	10	11	12	13
14	15	16	17	18	19	20
21	22	23	24	25	26	27
28	29	30	31	1	2	3

August
Su	Mo	Tu	We	Th	Fr	Sa
28	29	30	31	1	2	3
4	5	6	7	8	9	10
11	12	13	14	15	16	17
18	19	20	21	22	23	24
25	26	27	28	29	30	31

September
Su	Mo	Tu	We	Th	Fr	Sa
1	2	3	4	5	6	7
8	9	10	11	12	13	14
15	16	17	18	19	20	21
22	23	24	25	26	27	28
29	30	1	2	3	4	5

October
Su	Mo	Tu	We	Th	Fr	Sa
29	30	1	2	3	4	5
6	7	8	9	10	11	12
13	14	15	16	17	18	19
20	21	22	23	24	25	26
27	28	29	30	31	1	2

November
Su	Mo	Tu	We	Th	Fr	Sa
27	28	29	30	31	1	2
3	4	5	6	7	8	9
10	11	12	13	14	15	16
17	18	19	20	21	22	23
24	25	26	27	28	29	30

December
Su	Mo	Tu	We	Th	Fr	Sa
1	2	3	4	5	6	7
8	9	10	11	12	13	14
15	16	17	18	19	20	21
22	23	24	25	26	27	28
29	30	31	1	2	3	4

Daily planner

hourly schedule

Time	
6 AM	
7 AM	
8 AM	
9 AM	
10 AM	
11 AM	
12 PM	
1 PM	
2 PM	
3 PM	
4 PM	
5 PM	
6 PM	
7 PM	
8 PM	
9 PM	
10 PM	

Priorities

Work Plan

Personal Plan

Mood

Daily planner

hourly schedule

6 AM	
7 AM	
8 AM	
9 AM	
10 AM	
11 AM	
12 PM	
1 PM	
2 PM	
3 PM	
4 PM	
5 PM	
6 PM	
7 PM	
8 PM	
9 PM	
10 PM	

Priorities

Work Plan

Personal Plan

Mood

Daily planner

hourly schedule

6 AM	
7 AM	
8 AM	
9 AM	
10 AM	
11 AM	
12 PM	
1 PM	
2 PM	
3 PM	
4 PM	
5 PM	
6 PM	
7 PM	
8 PM	
9 PM	
10 PM	

Priorities

Work Plan

Personal Plan

Mood

hourly schedule

Time	
6 AM	
7 AM	
8 AM	
9 AM	
10 AM	
11 AM	
12 PM	
1 PM	
2 PM	
3 PM	
4 PM	
5 PM	
6 PM	
7 PM	
8 PM	
9 PM	
10 PM	

Priorities

Work Plan

Personal Plan

Mood

☺ 😄 😖 😐 😠

Daily planner

hourly schedule

Time	
6 AM	
7 AM	
8 AM	
9 AM	
10 AM	
11 AM	
12 PM	
1 PM	
2 PM	
3 PM	
4 PM	
5 PM	
6 PM	
7 PM	
8 PM	
9 PM	
10 PM	

Priorities

Work Plan

Personal Plan

Mood

😊 😄 😖 😐 😠

Daily planner

hourly schedule

6 AM	
7 AM	
8 AM	
9 AM	
10 AM	
11 AM	
12 PM	
1 PM	
2 PM	
3 PM	
4 PM	
5 PM	
6 PM	
7 PM	
8 PM	
9 PM	
10 PM	

Priorities

Work Plan

Personal Plan

Mood

Daily planner

hourly schedule

6 AM	
7 AM	
8 AM	
9 AM	
10 AM	
11 AM	
12 PM	
1 PM	
2 PM	
3 PM	
4 PM	
5 PM	
6 PM	
7 PM	
8 PM	
9 PM	
10 PM	

Priorities

Work Plan

Personal Plan

Mood

Daily planner

hourly schedule

Time	
6 AM	
7 AM	
8 AM	
9 AM	
10 AM	
11 AM	
12 PM	
1 PM	
2 PM	
3 PM	
4 PM	
5 PM	
6 PM	
7 PM	
8 PM	
9 PM	
10 PM	

Priorities

Work Plan

Personal Plan

Mood

hourly schedule

6 AM	
7 AM	
8 AM	
9 AM	
10 AM	
11 AM	
12 PM	
1 PM	
2 PM	
3 PM	
4 PM	
5 PM	
6 PM	
7 PM	
8 PM	
9 PM	
10 PM	

Priorities

Work Plan

Personal Plan

Mood

Daily planner

hourly schedule

Time	
6 AM	
7 AM	
8 AM	
9 AM	
10 AM	
11 AM	
12 PM	
1 PM	
2 PM	
3 PM	
4 PM	
5 PM	
6 PM	
7 PM	
8 PM	
9 PM	
10 PM	

Priorities

Work Plan

Personal Plan

Mood

☺ 😄 😟 😐 😠

hourly schedule

6 AM	
7 AM	
8 AM	
9 AM	
10 AM	
11 AM	
12 PM	
1 PM	
2 PM	
3 PM	
4 PM	
5 PM	
6 PM	
7 PM	
8 PM	
9 PM	
10 PM	

Priorities

Work Plan

Personal Plan

Mood

Daily planner

hourly schedule

6 AM	
7 AM	
8 AM	
9 AM	
10 AM	
11 AM	
12 PM	
1 PM	
2 PM	
3 PM	
4 PM	
5 PM	
6 PM	
7 PM	
8 PM	
9 PM	
10 PM	

Priorities

Work Plan

Personal Plan

Mood

Daily planner

hourly schedule

6 AM	
7 AM	
8 AM	
9 AM	
10 AM	
11 AM	
12 PM	
1 PM	
2 PM	
3 PM	
4 PM	
5 PM	
6 PM	
7 PM	
8 PM	
9 PM	
10 PM	

Priorities

Work Plan

Personal Plan

Mood

hourly schedule

6 AM	
7 AM	
8 AM	
9 AM	
10 AM	
11 AM	
12 PM	
1 PM	
2 PM	
3 PM	
4 PM	
5 PM	
6 PM	
7 PM	
8 PM	
9 PM	
10 PM	

Priorities

Work Plan

Personal Plan

Mood

Daily planner

hourly schedule

6 AM	
7 AM	
8 AM	
9 AM	
10 AM	
11 AM	
12 PM	
1 PM	
2 PM	
3 PM	
4 PM	
5 PM	
6 PM	
7 PM	
8 PM	
9 PM	
10 PM	

Priorities

Work Plan

Personal Plan

Mood

😊 😄 😖 😐 😠

2022 January

						1 Sat
2 Sun	3 Mon	4 Tue	5 Wed	6 Thu	7 Fri	8 Sat
9 Sun	10 Mon	11 Tue	12 Wed	13 Thu	14 Fri	15 Sat
16 Sun	17 Mon	18 Tue	19 Wed	20 Thu	21 Fri	22 Sat
23 Sun	24 Mon	25 Tue	26 Wed	27 Thu	28 Fri	29 Sat
30 Sun	31 Mon					

Birthdays
this month

_____

_____

_____

Give thanks to the Lord for he is good; his love endures forever.
Psalm 107:1

Important Dates
to remember

_____

_____

_____

_____

_____

February 2022

		1 Tue	2 Wed	3 Thu	4 Fri	5 Sat
6 Sun	7 Mon	8 Tue	9 Wed	10 Thu	11 Fri	12 Sat
13 Sun	14 Mon	15 Tue	16 Wed	17 Thu	18 Fri	19 Sat
20 Sun	21 Mon	22 Tue	23 Wed	24 Thu	25 Fri	26 Sat
27 Sun	28 Mon					

Birthdays
this month

_____
_____
_____

I can do all things through him who strengthens me.
Phil. 4:13

Important Dates
to remember

_____
_____
_____
_____
_____
_____

March 2022

	1 Tue	2 Wed	3 Thu	4 Fri	5 Sat
6 Sun	7 Mon	8 Tue	9 Wed	10 Thu	11 Fri	12 Sat
13 Sun	14 Mon	15 Tue	16 Wed	17 Thu	18 Fri	19 Sat
20 Sun	21 Mon	22 Tue	23 Wed	24 Thu	25 Fri	26 Sat
27 Sun	28 Mon	29 Tue	30 Wed	31 Thu		

Birthdays *this month*

Important Dates *to remember*

Oh, taste and see that the Lord is good!
Psalm 34:8

April 2022

					Fri 1	Sat 2
Sun 3	Mon 4	Tue 5	Wed 6	Thu 7	Fri 8	Sat 9
Sun 10	Mon 11	Tue 12	Wed 13	Thu 14	Fri 15	Sat 16
Sun 17	Mon 18	Tue 19	Wed 20	Thu 21	Fri 22	Sat 23
Sun 24	Mon 25	Tue 26	Wed 27	Thu 28	Fri 29	Sat 30

Birthdays *this month*

_____

_____

_____

He shields all who take refuge in Him
Psalms 18:30

Important Dates *to remember*

_____

_____

_____

_____

_____

1 Sun	2 Mon	3 Tue	4 Wed	5 Thu	6 Fri	7 Sat
8 Sun	9 Mon	10 Tue	11 Wed	12 Thu	13 Fri	14 Sat
15 Sun	16 Mon	17 Tue	18 Wed	19 Thu	20 Fri	21 Sat
22 Sun	23 Mon	24 Tue	25 Wed	26 Thu	27 Fri	28 Sat
29 Sun	30 Mon	31 Tue				

Birthdays
this month

_____

_____

_____

Important Dates
to remember

_____

_____

_____

_____

_____

Mercy, unto you, and PEACE AND LOVE, BE Multiplied.
Jude 1:2

June 2022

				1 Wed	2 Thu	3 Fri	4 Sat
5 Sun	6 Mon	7 Tue	8 Wed	9 Thu	10 Fri	11 Sat
12 Sun	13 Mon	14 Tue	15 Wed	16 Thu	17 Fri	18 Sat
19 Sun	20 Mon	21 Tue	22 Wed	23 Thu	24 Fri	25 Sat
26 Sun	27 Mon	28 Tue	29 Wed	30 Thu		

Birthdays
this month

_____

_____

_____

For I know the plans I have for you, declares the Lord, plans for welfare and not for evil, to give you a future and a hope.
Jer. 29:11

Important Dates
to remember

_____

_____

_____

_____

_____

_____

July 2022

					1 Fri	2 Sat
3 Sun	4 Mon	5 Tue	6 Wed	7 Thu	8 Fri	9 Sat
10 Sun	11 Mon	12 Tue	13 Wed	14 Thu	15 Fri	16 Sat
17 Sun	18 Mon	19 Tue	20 Wed	21 Thu	22 Fri	23 Sat
24 Sun	25 Mon	26 Tue	27 Wed	28 Thu	29 Fri	30 Sat
31 Sun						

Birthdays this month

_____
_____

Trust in the LORD with all your heart, and do not lean on your own understanding. In all your ways acknowledge him, and he will make straight your paths.
Prov. 3:5&6

Important Dates to remember

_____
_____
_____
_____
_____

2022 August

	1 Mon	2 Tue	3 Wed	4 Thu	5 Fri	6 Sat
7 Sun	8 Mon	9 Tue	10 Wed	11 Thu	12 Fri	13 Sat
14 Sun	15 Mon	16 Tue	17 Wed	18 Thu	19 Fri	20 Sat
21 Sun	22 Mon	23 Tue	24 Wed	25 Thu	26 Fri	27 Sat
28 Sun	29 Mon	30 Tue	31 Wed			

Birthdays *this month*

Important Dates *to remember*

Being confident of this very thing, that He who has begun a good work in you will complete it until the day of Jesus Christ

Phil. 1:6

September 2022

					1 Thu	2 Fri	3 Sat
4 Sun	5 Mon	6 Tue	7 Wed	8 Thu	9 Fri	10 Sat
11 Sun	12 Mon	13 Tue	14 Wed	15 Thu	16 Fri	17 Sat
18 Sun	19 Mon	20 Tue	21 Wed	22 Thu	23 Fri	24 Sat
25 Sun	26 Mon	27 Tue	28 Wed	29 Thu	30 Fri	

Birthdays *this month*

_____

_____

_____

And we know that for those who love God all things work together for good, for those who are called according to his purpose.
Rom. 8:28

Important Dates *to remember*

_____

_____

_____

_____

_____

_____

October 2022

						1 Sat
2 Sun	3 Mon	4 Tue	5 Wed	6 Thu	7 Fri	8 Sat
9 Sun	10 Mon	11 Tue	12 Wed	13 Thu	14 Fri	15 Sat
16 Sun	17 Mon	18 Tue	19 Wed	20 Thu	21 Fri	22 Sat
23 Sun	24 Mon	25 Tue	26 Wed	27 Thu	28 Fri	29 Sat
30 Sun	31 Mon					

Birthdays *this month*

_____
_____
_____

What then shall we say to these things? If God is for us, who can be against us?
Rom. 8:31

Important Dates *to remember*

_____
_____
_____
_____
_____
_____

2022 November

		1 Tue	2 Wed	3 Thu	4 Fri	5 Sat
6 Sun	7 Mon	8 Tue	9 Wed	10 Thu	11 Fri	12 Sat
13 Sun	14 Mon	15 Tue	16 Wed	17 Thu	18 Fri	19 Sat
20 Sun	21 Mon	22 Tue	23 Wed	24 Thu	25 Fri	26 Sat
27 Sun	28 Mon	29 Tue	30 Wed			

Birthdays *this month*

_____

_____

_____

Delight yourself in the Lord, and he will give you the desires of your heart.
Psalm 37:4

Important Dates *to remember*

_____

_____

_____

_____

_____

_____

December 2022

	Sun	Mon	Tue	Wed	Thu	Fri	Sat
				1	2	3	
4	5	6	7	8	9	10	
11	12	13	14	15	16	17	
18	19	20	21	22	23	24	
25	26	27	28	29	30	31	

Birthdays *this month*

Important Dates *to remember*

Have I not commanded you? Be strong and courageous. Do not be afraid; do not be discouraged, for the Lord your God will be with you wherever you go.
Joshua 1:9

to do List

Tasks   **Priority**

- [ ] _____ ○○○○○
- [ ] _____ ○○○○○
- [ ] _____ ○○○○○
- [ ] _____ ○○○○○
- [ ] _____ ○○○○○
- [ ] _____ ○○○○○
- [ ] _____ ○○○○○
- [ ] _____ ○○○○○
- [ ] _____ ○○○○○
- [ ] _____ ○○○○○
- [ ] _____ ○○○○○
- [ ] _____ ○○○○○
- [ ] _____ ○○○○○
- [ ] _____ ○○○○○
- [ ] _____ ○○○○○

to do List

Tasks   **Priority**

☐ _____ ○○○○○
☐ _____ ○○○○○
☐ _____ ○○○○○
☐ _____ ○○○○○
☐ _____ ○○○○○
☐ _____ ○○○○○
☐ _____ ○○○○○
☐ _____ ○○○○○
☐ _____ ○○○○○
☐ _____ ○○○○○
☐ _____ ○○○○○
☐ _____ ○○○○○
☐ _____ ○○○○○
☐ _____ ○○○○○
☐ _____ ○○○○○
☐ _____ ○○○○○

to do List

Tasks   **Priority**

- ☐ _____ ○○○○○
- ☐ _____ ○○○○○
- ☐ _____ ○○○○○
- ☐ _____ ○○○○○
- ☐ _____ ○○○○○
- ☐ _____ ○○○○○
- ☐ _____ ○○○○○
- ☐ _____ ○○○○○
- ☐ _____ ○○○○○
- ☐ _____ ○○○○○
- ☐ _____ ○○○○○
- ☐ _____ ○○○○○
- ☐ _____ ○○○○○
- ☐ _____ ○○○○○
- ☐ _____ ○○○○○
- ☐ _____ ○○○○○

To do List

Tasks   **Priority**

☐ _____ ○○○○○
☐ _____ ○○○○○
☐ _____ ○○○○○
☐ _____ ○○○○○
☐ _____ ○○○○○
☐ _____ ○○○○○
☐ _____ ○○○○○
☐ _____ ○○○○○
☐ _____ ○○○○○
☐ _____ ○○○○○
☐ _____ ○○○○○
☐ _____ ○○○○○
☐ _____ ○○○○○
☐ _____ ○○○○○
☐ _____ ○○○○○
☐ _____ ○○○○○

to do List

Tasks **Priority**

☐ _____ ○○○○○
☐ _____ ○○○○○
☐ _____ ○○○○○
☐ _____ ○○○○○
☐ _____ ○○○○○
☐ _____ ○○○○○
☐ _____ ○○○○○
☐ _____ ○○○○○
☐ _____ ○○○○○
☐ _____ ○○○○○
☐ _____ ○○○○○
☐ _____ ○○○○○
☐ _____ ○○○○○
☐ _____ ○○○○○
☐ _____ ○○○○○
☐ _____ ○○○○○

to do List

Tasks		Priority
☐ _____		○○○○○
☐ _____		○○○○○
☐ _____		○○○○○
☐ _____		○○○○○
☐ _____		○○○○○
☐ _____		○○○○○
☐ _____		○○○○○
☐ _____		○○○○○
☐ _____		○○○○○
☐ _____		○○○○○
☐ _____		○○○○○
☐ _____		○○○○○
☐ _____		○○○○○
☐ _____		○○○○○
☐ _____		○○○○○
☐ _____		○○○○○

to do List

Tasks **Priority**

☐ _____ ○○○○○
☐ _____ ○○○○○
☐ _____ ○○○○○
☐ _____ ○○○○○
☐ _____ ○○○○○
☐ _____ ○○○○○
☐ _____ ○○○○○
☐ _____ ○○○○○
☐ _____ ○○○○○
☐ _____ ○○○○○
☐ _____ ○○○○○
☐ _____ ○○○○○
☐ _____ ○○○○○
☐ _____ ○○○○○
☐ _____ ○○○○○
☐ _____ ○○○○○

To do List

Tasks	Priority
☐ _____	○○○○○
☐ _____	○○○○○
☐ _____	○○○○○
☐ _____	○○○○○
☐ _____	○○○○○
☐ _____	○○○○○
☐ _____	○○○○○
☐ _____	○○○○○
☐ _____	○○○○○
☐ _____	○○○○○
☐ _____	○○○○○
☐ _____	○○○○○
☐ _____	○○○○○
☐ _____	○○○○○
☐ _____	○○○○○
☐ _____	○○○○○

to do List

Tasks   **Priority**

- [ ] _____ ○○○○○
- [ ] _____ ○○○○○
- [ ] _____ ○○○○○
- [ ] _____ ○○○○○
- [ ] _____ ○○○○○
- [ ] _____ ○○○○○
- [ ] _____ ○○○○○
- [ ] _____ ○○○○○
- [ ] _____ ○○○○○
- [ ] _____ ○○○○○
- [ ] _____ ○○○○○
- [ ] _____ ○○○○○
- [ ] _____ ○○○○○
- [ ] _____ ○○○○○
- [ ] _____ ○○○○○
- [ ] _____ ○○○○○

to do List

Tasks   **Priority**

- [ ] _____ ○○○○○
- [ ] _____ ○○○○○
- [ ] _____ ○○○○○
- [ ] _____ ○○○○○
- [ ] _____ ○○○○○
- [ ] _____ ○○○○○
- [ ] _____ ○○○○○
- [ ] _____ ○○○○○
- [ ] _____ ○○○○○
- [ ] _____ ○○○○○
- [ ] _____ ○○○○○
- [ ] _____ ○○○○○
- [ ] _____ ○○○○○
- [ ] _____ ○○○○○
- [ ] _____ ○○○○○
- [ ] _____ ○○○○○

to do List

Tasks   **Priority**

- [ ] _____ ○○○○○
- [ ] _____ ○○○○○
- [ ] _____ ○○○○○
- [ ] _____ ○○○○○
- [ ] _____ ○○○○○
- [ ] _____ ○○○○○
- [ ] _____ ○○○○○
- [ ] _____ ○○○○○
- [ ] _____ ○○○○○
- [ ] _____ ○○○○○
- [ ] _____ ○○○○○
- [ ] _____ ○○○○○
- [ ] _____ ○○○○○
- [ ] _____ ○○○○○
- [ ] _____ ○○○○○
- [ ] _____ ○○○○○

To do List

Tasks		Priority
☐ _____		○○○○○
☐ _____		○○○○○
☐ _____		○○○○○
☐ _____		○○○○○
☐ _____		○○○○○
☐ _____		○○○○○
☐ _____		○○○○○
☐ _____		○○○○○
☐ _____		○○○○○
☐ _____		○○○○○
☐ _____		○○○○○
☐ _____		○○○○○
☐ _____		○○○○○
☐ _____		○○○○○
☐ _____		○○○○○
☐ _____		○○○○○

to do List

Tasks   **Priority**

- [ ] _____ ○○○○○
- [ ] _____ ○○○○○
- [ ] _____ ○○○○○
- [ ] _____ ○○○○○
- [ ] _____ ○○○○○
- [ ] _____ ○○○○○
- [ ] _____ ○○○○○
- [ ] _____ ○○○○○
- [ ] _____ ○○○○○
- [ ] _____ ○○○○○
- [ ] _____ ○○○○○
- [ ] _____ ○○○○○
- [ ] _____ ○○○○○
- [ ] _____ ○○○○○
- [ ] _____ ○○○○○
- [ ] _____ ○○○○○

To do List

Tasks   **Priority**

- [ ] _____ ○○○○○
- [ ] _____ ○○○○○
- [ ] _____ ○○○○○
- [ ] _____ ○○○○○
- [ ] _____ ○○○○○
- [ ] _____ ○○○○○
- [ ] _____ ○○○○○
- [ ] _____ ○○○○○
- [ ] _____ ○○○○○
- [ ] _____ ○○○○○
- [ ] _____ ○○○○○
- [ ] _____ ○○○○○
- [ ] _____ ○○○○○
- [ ] _____ ○○○○○
- [ ] _____ ○○○○○

notes

notes

notes

notes

notes

notes

notes

notes

notes

notes

notes

notes

notes

notes

notes

Setting goals

What is your goal?

When do you Plan to Start?

What is the time frame for you to reach this goal?

Why is this goal important to me?

What steps do I need to achieve the goal?

Is the goal realistic and obtainable?

What are some potential obstacles?

Do you Have a resolution in place?

Do you have a team?

What resources will you need?

Notes

Setting goals

What is your goal?

When do you Plan to Start?

What is the time frame for you to reach this goal?

Why is this goal important to me?

What steps do I need to achieve the goal?

Is the goal realistic and obtainable?

What are some potential obstacles?

Do you Have a resolution in place?

Do you have a team?

What resources will you need?

Notes

Setting goals

What is your goal?

When do you Plan to Start?

What is the time frame for you to reach this goal?

Why is this goal important to me?

What steps do I need to achieve the goal?

Is the goal realistic and obtainable?

What are some potential obstacles?

Do you Have a resolution in place?

Do you have a team?

What resources will you need?

Notes

Setting goals

What is your goal?

When do you Plan to Start?

What is the time frame for you to reach this goal?

Why is this goal important to me?

What steps do I need to achieve the goal?

Is the goal realistic and obtainable?

What are some potential obstacles?

Do you Have a resolution in place?

Do you have a team?

What resources will you need?

Notes

Setting goals

What is your goal?

When do you Plan to Start?

What is the time frame for you to reach this goal?

Why is this goal important to me?

What steps do I need to achieve the goal?

Is the goal realistic and obtainable?

What are some potential obstacles?

Do you Have a resolution in place?

Do you have a team?

What resources will you need?

Notes

Setting goals

What is your goal?

When do you Plan to Start?

What is the time frame for you to reach this goal?

Why is this goal important to me?

What steps do I need to achieve the goal?

Is the goal realistic and obtainable?

What are some potential obstacles?

Do you Have a resolution in place?

Do you have a team?

What resources will you need?

Notes

Setting goals

What is your goal?

When do you Plan to Start?

What is the time frame for you to reach this goal?

Why is this goal important to me?

What steps do I need to achieve the goal?

Is the goal realistic and obtainable?

What are some potential obstacles?

Do you Have a resolution in place?

Do you have a team?

What resources will you need?

Notes

Setting goals

What is your goal?

When do you Plan to Start?

What is the time frame for you to reach this goal?

Why is this goal important to me?

What steps do I need to achieve the goal?

Is the goal realistic and obtainable?

What are some potential obstacles?

Do you Have a resolution in place?

Do you have a team?

What resources will you need?

Notes

Setting goals

What is your goal?

When do you Plan to Start?

What is the time frame for you to reach this goal?

Why is this goal important to me?

What steps do I need to achieve the goal?

Is the goal realistic and obtainable?

What are some potential obstacles?

Do you Have a resolution in place?

Do you have a team?

What resources will you need?

Notes

Setting goals

What is your goal?

When do you Plan to Start?

What is the time frame for you to reach this goal?

Why is this goal important to me?

What steps do I need to achieve the goal?

Is the goal realistic and obtainable?

What are some potential obstacles?

Do you Have a resolution in place?

Do you have a team?

What resources will you need?

Notes

Setting goals

What is your goal?

When do you Plan to Start?

What is the time frame for you to reach this goal?

Why is this goal important to me?

What steps do I need to achieve the goal?

Is the goal realistic and obtainable?

What are some potential obstacles?

Do you Have a resolution in place?

Do you have a team?

What resources will you need?

Notes

Setting goals

What is your goal?

When do you Plan to Start?

What is the time frame for you to reach this goal?

Why is this goal important to me?

What steps do I need to achieve the goal?

Is the goal realistic and obtainable?

What are some potential obstacles?

Do you Have a resolution in place?

Do you have a team?

What resources will you need?

Notes

Setting goals

What is your goal?

When do you Plan to Start?

What is the time frame for you to reach this goal?

Why is this goal important to me?

What steps do I need to achieve the goal?

Is the goal realistic and obtainable?

What are some potential obstacles?

Do you Have a resolution in place?

Do you have a team?

What resources will you need?

Notes

Setting goals

What is your goal?

When do you Plan to Start?

What is the time frame for you to reach this goal?

Why is this goal important to me?

What steps do I need to achieve the goal?

Is the goal realistic and obtainable?

What are some potential obstacles?

Do you Have a resolution in place?

Do you have a team?

What resources will you need?

Notes

Setting goals

What is your goal?

When do you Plan to Start?

What is the time frame for you to reach this goal?

Why is this goal important to me?

What steps do I need to achieve the goal?

Is the goal realistic and obtainable?

What are some potential obstacles?

Do you Have a resolution in place?

Do you have a team?

What resources will you need?

Notes

Picture your Vision Here

Cut & Paste Pictures of your Goals & Dreams

Picture your Vision Here

Cut & Paste Pictures of your Goals & Dreams

Picture your Vision Here

Cut & Paste Pictures of your Goals & Dreams

Picture your Vision Here

Cut & Paste Pictures of your Goals & Dreams

Picture your Vision Here

Cut & Paste Pictures of your Goals & Dreams

Picture your Vision Here

Cut & Paste Pictures of your Goals & Dreams

Picture your Vision Here

Cut & Paste Pictures of your Goals & Dreams

Picture your Vision Here

Cut & Paste Pictures of your Goals & Dreams

Picture your Vision Here

Cut & Paste Pictures of your Goals & Dreams

Picture your Vision Here

Cut & Paste Pictures of your Goals & Dreams

Picture your Vision Here

Cut & Paste Pictures of your Goals & Dreams

Picture your Vision Here

Cut & Paste Pictures of your Goals & Dreams

Picture your Vision Here

Cut & Paste Pictures of your Goals & Dreams

Picture your Vision Here

Cut & Paste Pictures of your Goals & Dreams

Picture your Vision Here

Cut & Paste Pictures of your Goals & Dreams

Picture your Vision Here

Cut & Paste Pictures of your Goals & Dreams

Picture your Vision Here

Cut & Paste Pictures of your Goals & Dreams

Picture your Vision Here

Cut & Paste Pictures of your Goals & Dreams

Picture your Vision Here

Cut & Paste Pictures of your Goals & Dreams

Picture your Vision Here

Cut & Paste Pictures of your Goals & Dreams

Picture your Vision Here

Cut & Paste Pictures of your Goals & Dreams

www.ingramcontent.com/pod-product-compliance
Lightning Source LLC
Chambersburg PA
CBHW081359290426
44110CB00018B/2416